CHINESE EUNUCHS **I**

Inside Stories of the Chinese Court

太監傳奇

ASIAPAC COMIC SERIES

CHINESE EUNUCHS I

Inside Stories of the Chinese Court

太監傳奇

Conceived by
Wang Yongsheng and Chi Sheng

Illustrated by
Tian Hengyu

Translated by
Yang Aiwen, Gong Lizeng
and Wang Xingzheng

ASIAPAC • SINGAPORE

Publisher
ASIAPAC BOOKS PTE LTD
629 Aljunied Road #04-06
Cititech Industrial Building
Singapore 1438
Tel: 7453868
Fax: 7453822

First published March 1994

© ASIAPAC BOOKS, 1994
ISBN 981-3029-17-X

Cover design by Bay Song Lin
Typeset by Quaser Technology Pte Ltd
Body text in 8/9 pt Helvetica
Printed in Singapore by
Chung Printing

Publisher's Note

CHINESE EUNUCHS BOOK I, the first in a series of three, is about a group of very influential eunuchs in the Chinese courts. It features eunuchs from the Spring and Autumn period to the Eastern Han dynasty.

Since little is known about them in most books of history, this comic version offers light-hearted, invaluable insights into their lives and influence in old China. Find out how they schemed to get power and authority, and how they wrought deeds of corruption in the courts.

We are pleased to present the work of Tian Hengyu, a cartoonist from Mainland China, whose cartoons have been featured in numerous magazines and honoured among the best ten cartoon creations in China.

We would like to thank Yang Aiwen, Gong Lizeng and Wang Xingzheng for translating this volume and the production team for putting in their best effort in the publication of this book.

Chinese Eunuch Series:

Book I : Spring and Autumn Period to Eastern Han Dynasty
Book II : Tang to Song Dynasty
Book III : Ming to Qing Dynasty

About the Chinese Editors

Born in 1931, Wang Yongsheng has long been associated with the publishing industry. He has held many executive positions related to books, from distributor to publisher, from manager to editor-in-chief to director. He has also written essays, short stories and monographs, and drawn cartoons. In recent years, he has devoted most of his time to promoting comics, with the aim of reforming and further developing China's traditional comic art. He is now chairman of the Institute of Comic Books, a division of the Chinese Association of Oriental Cultural Studies.

Born in 1944, Chi Sheng has a Master of Medicine Science and has published a number of essays on medical genetics. But his interest in Chinese history and classical literature, in which he has also high attainments, is as notable as his achievements in medical science. To him, editing *Chinese Eunuchs* is a small test of his ability.

About the Translators

Yang Aiwen, Gong Lizeng and Wang Xingzheng are senior translators at the Morning Glory Publishers in Beijing, China. All three have been doing translation work for years, especially the translation of books on Chinese culture, art and history.

About the Illustrator

Born in Hejian county, Hebei province in 1941, Tian Hengyu published his first cartoons when he was only a middle school student. He stopped drawing cartoons for nearly 20 years after leaving school but took up art again in the late 70s.

His works cover a wide range of themes: ancient and modern, Chinese and foreign. They have appeared in more than 30 magazines. One of his cartoon strips, *Unofficial Biographies of Two Fools*, was serialized in the China Picture Story magazine for several years and honoured as one of the 10 best cartoon creations. It received an award for excellence for both text and pictures. Another work of his, *Dictionary of Idioms (Humorous Edition)*, is also a great hit.

Introduction

Taijian (eunuch), a word that often connotes a pervert, first appeared in the Chinese language about a thousand years ago. They were deemed suitable candidates for the emperor's close aides and attendants because they possessed both a masculine physique and a feminine docility. Still more important was that using men deprived of their reproductive power and sexual desires would safeguard the moral purity and sanctity of an emperor's private chambers. Therefore, as imperial power and autocracy increased, the use of castrated men to fill various male jobs in a palace gradually became a necessity.

Zhao Gao was the first eunuch in Chinese history to acquire supreme power. He won the favour of *Qin Shihuang* (the first emperor of Qin) and upon the latter's death seized control of the government even though he was only the prime minister.

Eunuchs did not have any real power during the Western Han dynasty. By the Eastern Han, however, they were given important posts such as *Changshi* (the emperor's close aide) and *Huangmen* (palace officials). The last emperors of the Eastern Han were only minors when they succeeded to the throne. Power was in the hands of their maternal relatives. When they reached maturity and tried to regain power, they had to rely on the eunuchs to stage palace coups. This gave the latter the opportunity to perform some "meritorious service" and thereby seize power. For close to thirty years, eunuchs were in control in the Eastern Han court and the chaos created by their misrule eventually caused the people to rebel.

During the Tang dynasty, Emperor Gaozong created a *Zhongyufu* (central imperial office) staffed by eunuchs called *Dajian* (senior eunuch) and *Shaojian* (junior eunuch), which helped to establish a eunuch hierarchy. Gao Lishi, a eunuch and favourite of Emperor Xuanzong, was made *Biaoqi jiangjun* (a military officer equivalent to a commander-in-chief whose authority was nominally second only to the prime minister), but he received only honours from the emperor and never did any real mischief.

The worst began in the reign of Emperor Suzong, who made Yu Chao'en, a eunuch, the highest ranking army supervisor, called *Guanjun Rongshi*. The appointment set a bad precedent of letting eunuchs advise and direct army commanders. Nearly all of the Tang emperors after Suzong were weak and incompetent. The eunuchs took advantage of this and wielded power despotically. They even had the final say in the enthronement and dethronement of emperors. Seven Tang emperors after Suzong were chosen by eunuchs and four brutally murdered.

Zhu Yuanzhang, founder of the Ming dynasty, knew well the tragic lessons of eunuchs wrecking the country. He therefore adopted a policy of "keeping eunuchs ignorant". Eunuchs were not allowed to learn how to read and write, nor to hold official titles. He even had an iron plate put up in the palace with the inscription "Inner palace officials (meaning eunuchs) are not allowed to interfere in court affairs; violators will be executed". He further decreed that these measures were to be enforced through all generations to come. His sons and grandsons, however, disregarded his orders, and the tragedy of eunuchs wrecking the country was soon reenacted in its worst form.

His son, Emperor Chenzu, took the lead in abolishing the measures that had restrained the power of eunuchs. Later, Emperor Wuzong abetted the crimes of Liu Jin, a eunuch whose cruelty and despotism were quite unprecedented. During Emperor Xizong's reign, Eunuch Wei Zhongxian held power far above that of the emperor.

The eunuch system of the Ming dynasty was a very comprehensive one. It had control over a total of twenty-four government offices, each headed by a eunuch who had custody of the office seal. The power of the eunuchs extended into almost every sphere of government activity, from the dispatch of envoys abroad, supervision of the armed forces, establishment of local garrisons, to espionage against both officials and the common people. Eunuch despotism ushered in a dark new age which of course hastened the downfall of the Ming.

The rulers of Qing were aware of the dangers of eunuch despotism and took measures to reduce the number and power of eunuchs. They placed the eunuchs under the control of the *Neiwufu* (a department in charge of political affairs in the imperial court) and decreed that eunuchs may not participate in court affairs nor hold official titles above the fourth rank. But Empress Dowager Cixi usurped power towards the end of the dynasty and this gave ambitious eunuchs such as An Dehai and Li Lianying the opportunity they needed to come to the fore.

It would not be fair to say that all eunuchs were bad. Quite a few of them were people of vision who served their country well. During the Warring States period, the king of Qin once demanded that the king of Zhao give him a valuable piece of jade in exchange for fifteen Qin cities. The king of Zhao distrusted the king of Qin but was afraid to incur his wrath. Eunuch Lao Xian recommended Lin Xiangru as Zhao's envoy to negotiate the exchange. Lin Xiangru handled the matter so skilfully that he saved both the honour of Zhao and its priceless relic. Cai Lun of the Eastern Han, who invented paper, and Zheng He of the early Ming, who made seven long voyages to distant countries, a remarkable achievement in Chinese naval and diplomatic history, were also eunuchs.

In the beginning, eunuchs were just a low class of palace attendants, the victims of the extravagant and licentious way of life of kings and emperors. They had to learn to obey the emperor's slightest wish and indulge his every whim in order to please and survive. These circumstances forced them to cultivate a slave mentality, a point on which they deserved some compassion. On the other hand, being the lackeys of an autocrat with unlimited power, eunuchs could do things ordinary people were incapable of doing. When they grasped real power, they would often use it with disastrous effects. Because of the great physical sacrifice a eunuch had to make, he was prone to seek compensation many times over for what he had lost. This twisted state of mind accounted for a eunuch's inordinate lust for power, revenge, cruelty and enjoyment.

Together with the end of the feudal dynasties, eunuchs too, have disappeared like funerary objects buried with the dead. However, both eunuchs and the eunuch system had existed for a long time in Chinese history and the retrogressive roles they played at certain stages cannot be ignored.

So many eunuchs have appeared in history but many of the stories are similar. We have therefore selected a number of representative characters whose stories will give the reader a general idea of these people and their unsavoury activities. There were three peaks of eunuch trouble in Chinese history : the Eastern Han, Tang and Ming dynasties. Our selections are mainly from these three periods.

Every story in this book is about a real man and real events. We did our best to represent history in its true form, but since this is a comic series and not a history textbook, we cannot dispense with characteristics essential to comics such as humour, exaggeration and occasional jokes that do not affect the main course of events. Another point that should be noted is that, since this book is intended for the present generation, certain ancient ways of writing and speaking have been translated into their modern equivalents. Of course, some historical expressions that are not difficult to understand have been preserved in their original form.

It is hoped that this introduction and the selections we have made will be informative to our readers.

Contents

Spring and Autumn Period
Shu Diao 豎刁

(? – 642BC)

In 685 BC, Xiaobai became the ruler of Qi under the title Duke Huan. Assisted by his chief minister, Guan Zhong, and capable officials, Bao Shuya and Xi Peng, Qi became strong and prosperous. In 681 BC, he summoned the rulers of other feudal states to a meeting at Beixing (now Dong'e County, Shandong Province), at which he was chosen to be the chief of a great political alliance. Elated by success, the duke led his armies in triumph back to Linzi, his capital, where in the privacy of his palace our story of Eunuch Shu Diao begins...

Yao-Shun: Yao and Shun were idealized emperors of ancient China.

2

4

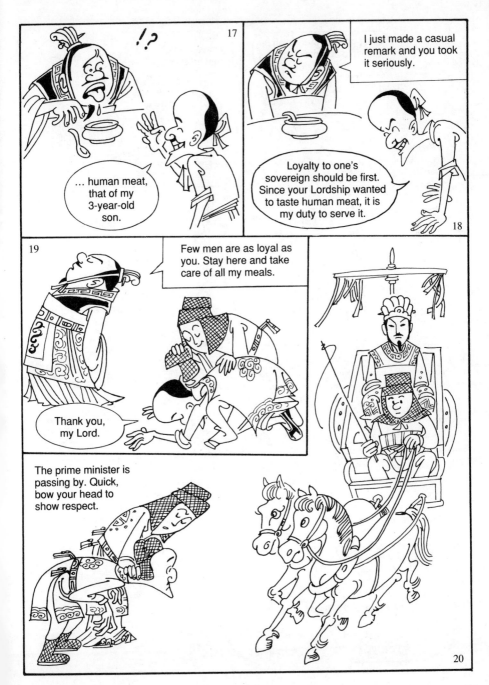

5

In 645 BC, Guan Zhong was critically ill. Duke Huan went to see him.

Who can be my prime minister after you?

Xi Peng.

33

How about your friend Bao Shuya?

34

He can, but he's not tolerant enough and that's a drawback.

Can Shu Diao, Yi Ya and Kai Fang be used?

35

No, they're villains. You must get rid of them when I'm gone, or the country will be in chaos.

Why didn't you tell me this earlier?

Because they know how to please you. These 3 men are like flood waters, and I'm the dike holding them back. But I will soon be gone, so you must take preventive measures immediately.

36

Have you heard the news? Guan Zhong is dying and he wants the duke to get rid of us.

Xi Peng looks ill, he won't live long.

Let's throw in with Bao Shuya and stab Guan Zhong in the back.

9

37

You let Guan Zhong be prime minister, but he didn't recommend you to succeed him. That's very unfair!

Guan Zhong once deserted the duke. It was your Excellency who pleaded for his pardon.

And it was your Excellency who first assisted Duke Huan in governing the country.

38

I want to be the minister of justice and arrest you traitors. Get out!

39

Xi Peng became prime minister after Guan Zhong's death, but he died a month later.

Both Uncle Zhong and Xi Peng are gone. Bao Shuya, you must accept the post of prime minister.

You must expel the "influential trio" before I accept the post.

At Bao Shuya's insistence, Duke Huan sent the "influential trio" out of Linzi.

Too bad, you must go.

40

With tears in his eyes, Yi Ya took leave of his mistress, the Elder Weiji, one of Duke Huan's concubines.

41

Honey, our only hope of reunion rests with you.

You go first. I'll ...

Darling, I just can't leave you!

40

42

43

44

You've called back Yi Ya. Have you forgotten Uncle Zhong's last words?

These 3 men are useful to me and harmless to the state. We needn't listen to everything Uncle Zhong said.

45

Good-ness!

Bao Shuya vomited blood on returning home that day and died last night.

Who will assist me from now on?

With the death of Bao Shuya, the last "dike" to prevent "flood waters" was gone.

We are back again!

46

Now that Bao Shuya has died, we have the final say in everything.

Yes, from now on we can hold our heads high.

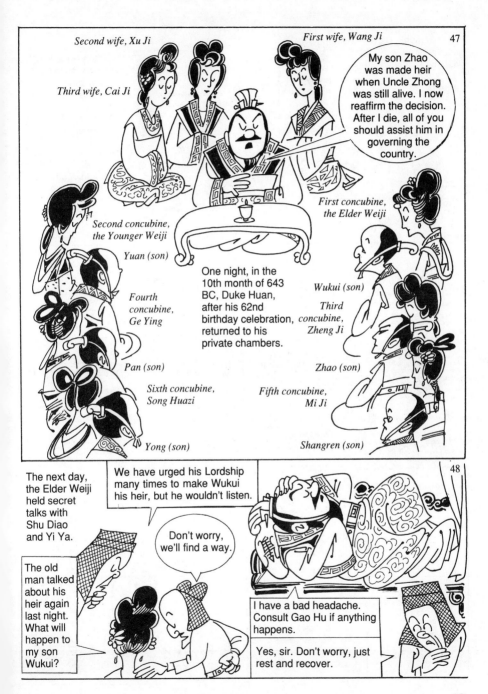

14

15

71 Your Lordship .... forgive us for not fulfilling our duty ...

72 Numskulls!

73 Guard the palace gate well. If any of the late duke's sons dare come in, kill him.

74 The late duke's son, Pan, is the rightful heir. If anyone doubts this, let him ask this sword of mine.

Kai Fang led his servants to guard the East Hall and installed Pan as duke.

75 Yuan, another of the late duke's sons, occupied the West Hall.

I, Shangren, pledge to succeed my father as duke, a right I'll never relinquish.

I wouldn't raise any objections to Zhao's right as heir. But since he's gone, I have as much right as any of the others.

Meanwhile, Shangren, another son of Duke Huan, massed his troops outside the palace.

76

All the brothers are deploying their troops. What shall we do?

None of them has an edge over the others. It's not yet time for a showdown.

We have the late duke's body, and that makes us the orthodox party.

77

The fight for power among the sons of Duke Huan was deadlocked for over 2 months, during which the duke's body lay exposed. Though it was winter, the body rotted. Duke Huan, the greatest of the "5 Overlords of the Spring and Autumn Period," who headed an alliance of dukes all his life, never imagined he would come to such an ignominious end.

If you preside over the funeral, we'll support you as heir.

With the duke's body still laying in the open, can your Lordship feel at ease?

78

You two decide.

79

Through the mediation of Gao Hu and Guo Yizhong, Duke Huan's body was finally buried.

80

19

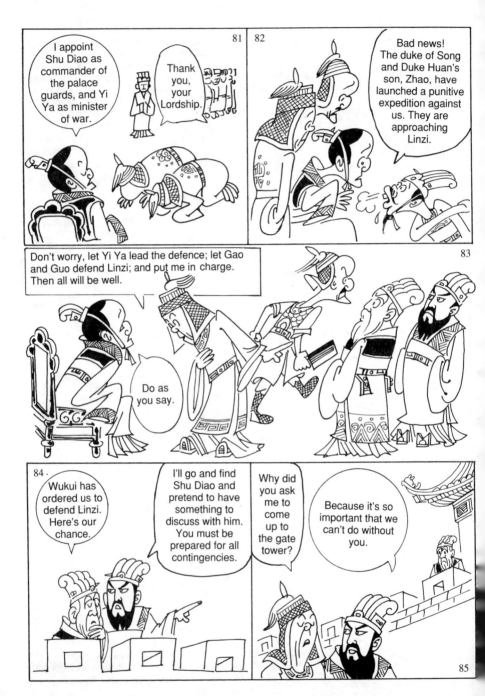

20

21

Qin Dynasty

Zhao Gao 趙高

(? – 207BC)

Horse

1 Zhao Gao was castrated when young. Shrewd by nature, physically strong, and good at interpreting criminal laws, he was regarded highly by *Qin Shihuang** and became the tutor of the emperor's younger son, Hu Hai.

The laws of Qin are the hairs on the head of *Qin Shihuang.*

Teacher, did I do well in the last exam?

Yes. I'll recommend to the emperor that you be handsomely rewarded.

2

In the last years of the reign of *Qin Shihuang,* Zhao Gao was promoted to *Zhongchefuling**.

The emperor is going to the imperial ancestral temple tomorrow. Get 50 vehicles ready.

I'm going to tour the country. You three come along and take care of the vehicles, horses and baggages.

Yes, Your Majesty.

3

4

In the winter of 211 BC, *Qin Shihuang* made an inspection tour of the country, taking with him his prime minister, Li Si, son, Hu Hai, and Zhao Gao.

During his journey, *Qin Shihuang* showed off his imperial power. He held sacrificial ceremonies for Shun, the legendary monarch of Yu, at Yunmeng and for Yu the Great in Kuaiji. At Langya, he sent Xu Fu out to sea to seek the elixir of life and at Zhifu, he killed a giant fish.

5

Qin Shihuang: *The first emperor of Qin.*

24 ***Zhongchefuling:*** *An official who had custody of the imperial seal and directed the issue and execution of imperial mandates, and also had control over the use of imperial vehicles.*

6

I'll not live long. Send word to Crown Prince Fu Su to hand over his command to Meng Tian and return at once to Xianyang to preside over my funeral and succeed to the throne ...

In the autumn of 210 BC, *Qin Shihuang* fell seriously ill while on tour in Pingyuanjin. Knowing that he was dying, he hastened to make his last will.

8

We must not let anyone know of this lest it should cause disturbances.

The imperial seal and the emperor's last will are with me. Old fellow, you just wait and see.

Rest assured, prime minister, it'll be kept top secret.

Qin Shihuang died at Shaqiu on the way back to Xianyang. **7**

9

The emperor has just recovered and needs a good rest. If there is anything to be reported to him, let me do it. We must return to Xianyang quickly!

10

The emperor was very ill. How could he have recovered so quickly?

25

Langzhongling: An official in charge of all households at the two sides of the palace.

Don't worry, we are not afraid of death.

I begged the emperor to set you free. You must fight well.

36

37
Zhang Han has defeated the rebels!

This shows how wise your decision was.

38
Chen Sheng, the leader of the rebels, has been killed.

Ha! Ha! Just a few rebels after all!

39
I'll be in for it if someone were to complain about me to the emperor.

Zhang Han's victory saved Qin, but Zhao Gao was still uneasy because he had done so much evil.

40
I've got an idea.

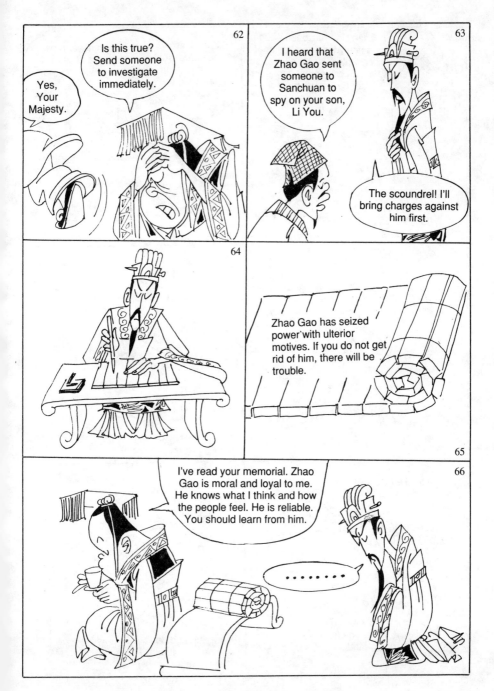

39

Taibu: An official in charge of divinations.

107

The emperor did as Zhao Gao suggested. He went to Wangyi Palace to fast again.

Stay here and fast. I'll go and get some beauties and rare objects to amuse you.

108

Brother, bad news! General Wang Li has been killed in battle, Zhang Han has surrendered and Liu Bang's army is approaching Xianyang ...

!!!

109

A secret envoy from Liu Bang is here to see you.

Let him in quickly and keep it a secret.

110

Our army is approaching Xianyang. The end of the Qin dynasty is near. What are you going to do, prime minister?

I've always wanted to serve General Liu. I'll assist from the inside.

111

This is a small gift to mark our first meeting. Later ...

I'm unworthy of it! Please put in a good word for me before General Liu.

49

Eastern Han Dynasty

Shan Chao 單超

(? – AD160)

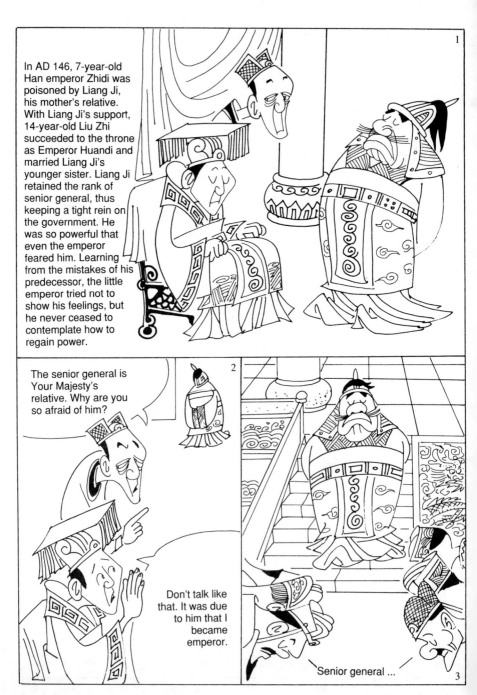

In AD 146, 7-year-old Han emperor Zhidi was poisoned by Liang Ji, his mother's relative. With Liang Ji's support, 14-year-old Liu Zhi succeeded to the throne as Emperor Huandi and married Liang Ji's younger sister. Liang Ji retained the rank of senior general, thus keeping a tight rein on the government. He was so powerful that even the emperor feared him. Learning from the mistakes of his predecessor, the little emperor tried not to show his feelings, but he never ceased to contemplate how to regain power.

The senior general is Your Majesty's relative. Why are you so afraid of him?

Don't talk like that. It was due to him that I became emperor.

Senior general ...

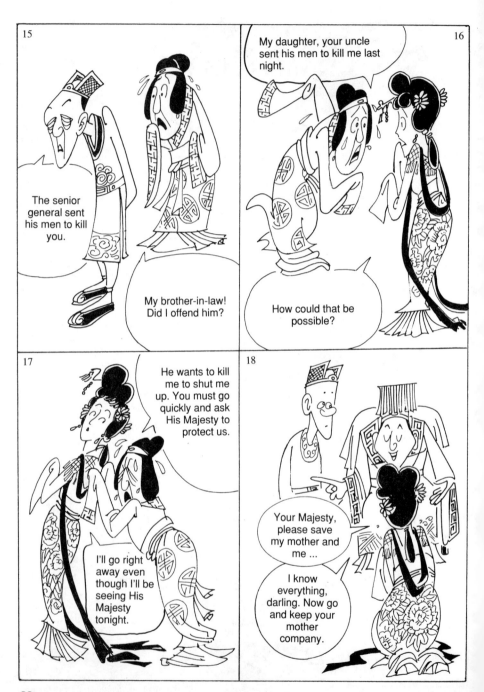

Zhongchangshi: A close aide to the emperor and empress whose duties were of a secretarial nature.
Xiaohuangmen: A eunuch of lower rank.

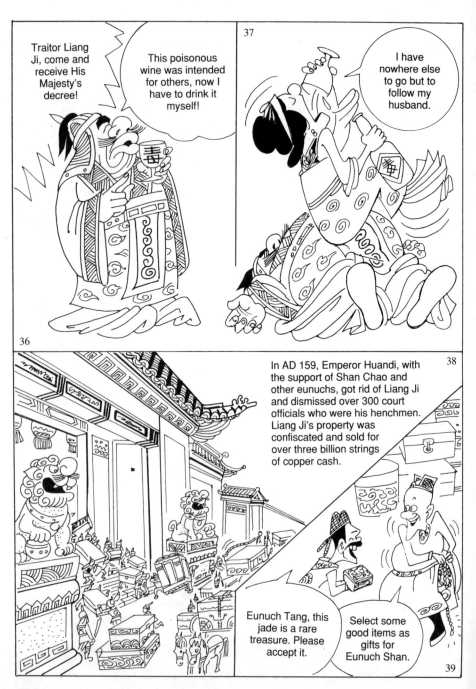

43 Liu Pu, Zhao Zhong and 6 other junior eunuchs should also be rewarded for their services in removing the traitors.

I grant each of them the title *Xianghou*.

44 Liu Pu, Zhao Zhong ... what are those for?

They're gifts from the 8 of us to show our gratitude.

After Shan Chao was made marquis of Xinfeng, he remembered his followers and relatives. His brother Shan An and nephew Shan Kuang, however, were too impatient and came to beg him for favours.

Now that you're rich and powerful, don't forget us.

Of course I won't. In fact, I've already arranged for Shan An to be prefect of Hedong and Shan Kuang, prefect of Jiyin.

45

46 Aren't those places very poor?

Hedong is noted for its hedgehog hydnum and Jiyin for its peonies. They are sources of wealth and also of strategic importance.

Xianghou: A marquis of secondary rank.

Cheqi jiangjun: An officer ranking just below the senior general.

71

My uncle, you may be rest assured. This man shan't drink a drop of Shuofang water.

Dear nephew Dong Yuan, Please execute the criminal Diwu Zhong as soon as he arrives ...

74

The king of hell appreciates your talent so much, he would like you to work in hell!

Shan Chao died of an illness in AD 160. To honour him, Emperor Huandi ordered jade articles to be buried with him, and a general and the deputy prime minister to lead the funeral procession of 2,000 people.

Eternal glory to Shan Chao!

75

76

After Shan Chao's death, the other eunuchs continued in their evil ways. Later, Xu Huang and Tang Heng died of illnesses while Zuo Guan committed suicide. Ju Yuan was dismissed for having offended Emperor Huandi and died at home.

Eastern Han Dynasty

Cao Jie 曹節

(? – AD181)

In AD 167, Emperor Huandi died. As he had no son, Senior General Dou Wu wanted his own daughter, Empress Dou, to be the regent. So he arranged for Liu Hong, a descendant of the imperial house who was only 12 years old, to succeed to the throne at the nomination of Liu Tiao, the censor. Liu Tiao and *Zhongchangshi* Cao Jie went to Hejian to escort the little emperor to the capital.

Liu Hong ascended the throne as Emperor Lingdi with Empress Dowager Dou as regent.

Cao Jie is hereby made marquis of Chang'an for his service in installing the new emperor.

Thank you, Your Highness.

This is Mrs Zhao, the emperor's wet nurse.

You are Zhao Rao? I like you. From now on, come and keep me company.

4. My brother wrote to say that ever since Your Highness became regent, the crops are better than before.

The morale of the people are better too.

5. Cao Jie, Zhao Rao and another *Zhongchangshi*, Wang Fu, conspired to ask the empress dowager to confer titles on many of their relatives and friends. For this they made out a long list.

A total of 446 people which included your adopted sons, Wang Ji and Wang Meng, my brother Cao Poshi and Mrs Zhao's cousin ...

Mrs Zhao, it's up to you now!

I'll give the empress dowager the list when she's in a good mood.

List of Names

6. The long list was soon approved and the new officials celebrated.

7. Wang Ji, you are illiterate yet you can become a prefect just because you're some important person's adopted son!

Cao Poshi, even a playboy like you can command an army? Ha! Ha!

8. The old official, Yang, accused me of seizing over 500 *qing** of land but it's not true. I bought the land in 3 instalments – it's just that I haven't paid for it yet.

Minister Zhang accused me of selling 86 women in a day. How could it be possible?

Don't worry, I know both of you are honest men.

Qing: A Chinese unit of area equivalent to 6.67 hectares.

81

9

The evildoings of Cao Jie, Wang Fu and their henchmen aroused widespread anger in the court. In AD 168, *Taifu** Chen Fan urged Senior General Dou Wu to get rid of Cao and Wang, but Empress Dowager Dou intervened and protected them. A palace coup ensued, resulting in the death of Chen Fan and Dou Wu. The empress dowager was placed under house arrest in the South Palace. Cao Jie and Wang Fu became even more powerful.

Cao Jie is hereby promoted to garrison commander of Changle Palace and marquis of Yuyang, and Wang Fu to *Huangmenling.**

10

Get rid of all who side with Chen Fan and Dou Wu ...

Right! You can't plant cabbages until the turnips are pulled out.

Appointments and Removals

General Zhang Huan, who did not know the truth about the palace intrigues, played a key role in defeating Dou Wu during the palace coup and thus was regarded as Cao Jie's man and amply rewarded.

Zhang Huan is hereby promoted to *Dasinong** for his service in removing traitors.

Imperial Decree

I've just had a heart attack ... and wouldn't dare to accept the appointment.

11

12

I've already read aloud the imperial decree. Be wise and do not defy orders.

.....

13

Why didn't you accept the post of *Dasinong*?

I was ignorant and helped the devil. What merit was there to speak of?

Taifu: An official ranking above the 3 chancellors in the Eastern Han dynasty.
Huangmenling: The chief of the eunuchs.
Dasinong: A minister in charge of land tax, money, grain, salt and iron, and of state revenue and expenditure.

Yao ying: *Sparrow hawk.*

89

Wang Fu's adopted son Wang Ji was prime minister of Peijun principality for 5 years. He was an extremely cruel man who delighted in torturing and killing people. No less than 10,000 people were killed. He enjoyed tearing a person apart using horse carts and displaying the dismembered body as a lesson for others. In summer, when the bodies of his victims rotted, he had them strung together and driven through the principality in open carts. The sight and smell was so revolting that people fled in terror.

46

47

Who is Yang Qiu? Come and meet me, Wang Biao.

Who dares block the minister's carriage?

How dare you! Arrest him!

News that Yang Qiu had arrested Wang Biao spread quickly in the capital. Yang Biao, the mayor, seized the opportunity to submit a memorial to the emperor, exposing the wrongdoings of Wang Fu and his sons.

Wang Fu's son, Wang Biao, with the connivance of his father, has extorted cash from the people but nobody dares to speak out.

I'm Wang Fu's adopted son! Who dares touch me?

Wang Ji killed over 10,000 people in Peijun and there's nobody left to pay taxes.

No wonder our coffers are empty. Arrest Wang Fu and his sons immediately.

48

49

94

71

Arrest them immediately! I'll interrogate them myself!

72

When will the emperor interrogate them?

There'll be no interrogation. Make their deaths look like suicide.

Cao Jie became prime minister after the incident but he felt no peace and lived in constant fear of being assassinated.

Assassin!

No, it's only the wind.

73

In AD 181, Cao Jie died. Emperor Lingdi, who had been hoodwinked by Cao Jie all along, granted him the posthumous title of *Cheqi jiangjun* in memory of him.

Cao Jie, *Cheqi jiangjun* of the Han dynasty.

74

Zhang Rang 張讓

(? – AD189)

During the reign of Emperor Lingdi of the Eastern Han dynasty, 2 eunuchs, called Zhang Rang and Zhao Zhong, won the emperor's favour and were affectionately addressed as *Ah Mu*** and *Ah Fu*** respectively. These 2 eunuchs and 10 others were granted the title of *Liehou***. They were also popularly referred to as the 10 *Changshi* although there were 12 of them.

Ah Fu and *Ah Mu,* I'm very worried about the disorder in the country.

With us in charge, Your Majesty has no cause for worry.

Zhang An, show me the list of gifts we received recently.

Yes, sir.

You've sent me gifts 8 times. What can I do for you?

Our respected chief administrator, I'm Meng Tuo, a merchant of Fufeng, and I've come to present you with this small gift.

Would you mind bowing down to me in public at the gate of your house?

Ah Mu: *Mother* **Ah Fu:** *Father*
Liehou: *The highest rank of the Eastern Han nobility.*
Changshi: *Same as Zhongchangshi.*

Meng Tuo was a shrewd merchant who knew all the tricks in business. He invested heavily and got high returns. Then he reinvested even more and got an even higher return.

990 taels of gold, 142 jade articles, 160 pieces of marten, 1,240 pieces of Korean ginseng ... I'll let Zhang An have a tenth of these, keep two tenth in reserve and send the rest to Zhang Rang ...

13

I've heard that you're a man of great wealth, and now I've seen it. The imperial court is looking for talent. I think you're the only person fit to take up the post of governor of Liangzhou.

Master Zhang, I'll never forget your kindness.

14

The 10 *Changshi* had halls, towers and pavilions built in their mansions that were more magnificent than those in the imperial palace. One day, Emperor Lingdi suddenly wanted to go up a high platform in Yongle Palace. Fearing that the emperor might see the halls and pavilions in his mansion, Zhang Rang told a lie to discourage the emperor.

Ah Fu, let's go up the platform to enjoy the view.

Your Majesty, it is beneath the dignity of an emperor to ascend so high and be seen by the common people.

15

101

Emperor Lingdi did not mount the platform and retained his "dignity"; nevertheless, the people rebelled because life had become unbearable. In AD 184, the Yellow Turban Rebellion broke out and won support from all over the country. The panic-stricken Emperor Lingdi hurriedly summoned his officials to a meeting.

General Huangfu Song, what should we do?

The indiscriminate executions of Party people* in recent years were unjust. To reassure the public, all such wrongs must be redressed.

16

What would you suggest, Lu Qiang?

Only when corrupt and treacherous officials are removed can there be peace and stability.

18

As a *Zhongchangshi*, Lu Qiang should be on our side, but he always speaks against us.

17

19

Lu Qiang is reading 'A Biography of Huo Guang'. He wants to follow Huo Guang's example and depose the emperor.

Humph! Get rid of him!

20

Master Lu, you always find fault with us. But now that you've offended His Majesty, we have to do our duty.

Lu Qiang tries to appeal for Li Ying because he and Li were sworn brothers.

I see. Put him in prison!

I expected this long ago.

Party people: A reference to members of an alliance led by Li Ying, an aristocrat, and some scholars of the Imperial College during the last years of the Eastern Han.

Shizhong: An assistant the prime minister who was allowed to enter and leave the palace freely.

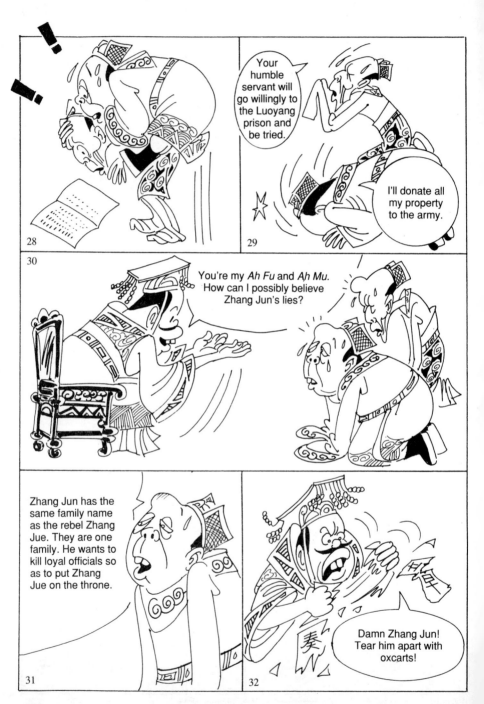

33

The Han court was badly shaken by the Yellow Turban uprising which was rapidly gaining support. Emperor Lingdi made Yang Ci his *Taiwei** and asked him how to quell the uprising. Yang Ci's words, however, infuriated the emperor.

Traitors within the courts must be removed before you can subjugate the rebels.

The same old talk! Go away!

35

Emperor Lingdi sent *Xiaohuangmen* Zuo Feng to inspect the forces commanded by Lu Zhi, captain of the imperial bodyguards, who was fighting the Yellow Turbans.

What local delicacies have you here? Get some for me.

But you must have some *yellow and white things**.

34

We have only sweet potato stalks in the army. Each soldier gets 200 grams of the stalks each day and has to look for bark and roots to keep himself from starving.

People who eat sweet potato stalks excrete only hard and black matters, no yellow or white.

Stingy Lu Zhi! You'll pay for it.

37

Your Majesty, Lu Zhi does nothing but drink and play chess. He said he would wait for the Yellow Turbans to be struck by lightning.

This is outrageous! Arrest him and bring him to the capital!

36

Taiwei: *A high military rank equivalent to the prime minister.*
Yellow and white things: *A veiled reference to gold and silver.*

105

38

General Lu, it's been a long time since we last met. I've told the jailer to prepare sweet potato stalks for you, 200 grams a day.

The Yellow Turbans were suppressed in AD 185, but then, a great fire reduced the magnificent Han palace to rubble.

Our coffers are empty ... Where can we get money to rebuild the palace?

That's easy. If we increase the land tax by just 10 copper coins per *mu**, there will be more than enough.

39

After Your Majesty issues the edict for land tax increase, the people will willingly contribute to the rebuilding of the palace.

You could issue another edict for the prefectures to donate their best timber and stone.

Good idea! You handle it.

40

41

The prefectures were ordered to deliver the tax money and building materials to the Western Garden, an imperial hunting ground controlled by eunuchs. This gave the eunuchs a chance to grab a large share for themselves.

I brought 30 cartloads of timber. Please open the gates and take them.

Pay the service charge first.

1 mu: *A Chinese unit of area, equivalent to 0.07 hectare.*

42

Cashier

Service Charge

Large prefecture:
30 million strings
of cash
Small prefecture:
15 million strings
of cash

This is a price list made out by senior economists. An official post with a salary of 400 *piculs** of grain costs 4 million strings of cash; a post with a salary of 2,000 *piculs* costs 20 million strings; ... This is quite reasonable: 10,000 strings for each *picul* of one's salary.

Price List

43

6 months have passed and we still haven't received all the money needed for rebuilding the palace.

In some prefectures, the people ran away, so no one paid.

44

I heard that the late Emperor Huandi collected good money by selling official posts. Can't I do the same?

Of course you can. You can evenrise the prices since everything costs more nowadays.

46

I love talent. How about letting people with talent pay half the amount?

Of course. They can even pay by instalments, say, within a year after they assume office, but the interest rate will be doubled.

45

1 picul: The equivalent of 133.33 pounds.

107

Your Lordship, here're 500 taels of gold and 300 jewels. Please accept them as a small gift from me. I'd like to buy an official post called pre ... er ...

My kind of business needs no capital. Ha! Ha!

You can be considered a man of talent and need pay only half the amount according to our terms.

Prefect, you mean. That can be easily arranged. But where did you get so much money when everyone else is poor?

Nego-tiation Table

47

48

49

The lives of the people became worse after the Yellow Turbans were crushed. This gave rise to more peasant uprisings. Among the notable peasant leaders were Zhang Niujiao of Boling, Chu Feiyan of Changshan, Lei Gong, Fu Yun, Bai Que, Yang Feng, Yu Du and Wu Lu ... Emperor Lingdi, however, was in the dark because Zhang Rang withheld all information from him.

Court Censor Liu Tao risked his life to make the following remarks.

Because of the wrongdoings of the eunuchs, who have deceived Your Majesty and done much harm to the people, the whole country is now in turmoil. It's high time Your Majesty dealt with these eunuchs!

50

Is what you said true?

108

111

61 His Majesty is sending me to the western frontier. This is one of Zhang Rang's tricks. His Majesty is ill and I'm afraid ...

My dear, you must not leave the capital. Pretend to be sick and stall for time.

62 My brother-in-law, I'm getting worse each day. I commit the Liu family's heritage to your care.

Please rest assured, Your Majesty.

63 I, Jian Shuo, pledge to be worthy of your trust.

My elder son Liu Bian was born by Empress He and has been made crown prince. My younger son Liu Xie was born by Wang Meiren. He is clever and likable, but Empress He may not like him, so take care of him.

64 Emperor Lingdi died in AD189 at age 33.

115

The empress dowager placed Zhang Rang under her protection after her mother and sister pleaded for him. However, the young officers, Yuan Shao and Cao Cao, saw the danger and were determined to get rid of the eunuchs.

Senior general, if you don't destroy them you will suffer for it someday.

Don't forget the example of Senior General Dou Wu.

Yes ... you're quite right ...

85

Zhao Zhong, call our men together immediately. Tell them to be armed and lie in ambush behind the palace gate. Guo Sheng, go and tell He Jin the empress dowager wants to see him.

He Jin entered and then left the palace in a hurry. Something is wrong. Bring Zhao Zhong here, quickly.

86

87

119

121

A Brief Chronology of Chinese History

夏 Xia Dynasty			About 2100 – 1600 BC
商 Shang Dynasty			About 1600 – 1100 BC
周 Zhou Dynasty	西周 Western Zhou Dynasty		About 1100 – 771 BC
	東周 Eastern Zhou Dynasty		770 – 256 BC
	春秋 Spring and Autumn Period		770 – 476 BC
	戰國 Warring States		475 – 221 BC
秦 Qin Dynasty			221 – 207 BC
漢 Han Dynasty	西漢 Western Han		206 BC – AD 24
	東漢 Eastern Han		25 – 220
三國 Three Kingdoms	魏 Wei		220 – 265
	蜀漢 Shu Han		221 – 263
	吳 Wu		222 – 280
西晉 Western Jin Dynasty			265 – 316
東晉 Eastern Jin Dynasty			317 – 420
南北朝 Northern and Southern Dynasties	南朝 Southern Dynasties	宋 Song	420 – 479
		齊 Qi	479 – 502
		梁 Liang	502 – 557
		陳 Chen	557 – 589
	北朝 Northern Dynasties	北魏 Northern Wei	386 – 534
		東魏 Eastern Wei	534 – 550
		北齊 Northern Qi	550 – 577
		西魏 Western Wei	535 – 556
		北周 Northern Zhou	557 – 581
隋 Sui Dynasty			581 – 618
唐 Tang Dynasty			618 – 907
五代 Five Dynasties	後梁 Later Liang		907 – 923
	後唐 Later Tang		923 – 936
	後晉 Later Jin		936 – 946
	後漢 Later Han		947 – 950
	後周 Later Zhou		951 – 960
宋 Song Dynasty	北宋 Northern Song Dynasty		960 – 1127
	南宋 Southern Song Dynasty		1127 – 1279
遼 Liao Dynasty			916 – 1125
金 Jin Dynasty			1115 – 1234
元 Yuan Dynasty			1271 – 1368
明 Ming Dynasty			1368 – 1644
清 Qing Dynasty			1644 – 1911
中華民國 Republic of China			1912 – 1949
中華人民共和國 People's Republic of China			1949 –

Strategy & Leadership Series by Wang Xuanming

Thirty-six Stratagems: Secret Art of War
Translated by Koh Kok Kiang (cartoons) &
Liu Yi (text of the stratagems)
    A Chinese military classic which emphasizes deceptive schemes to achieve military objectives. It has attracted the attention of military authorities and general readers alike.

Six Strategies for War: The Practice of Effective Leadership
Translated by Alan Chong
    A powerful book for rulers, administrators and leaders, it covers critical areas in management and warfare including: how to recruit talents and manage the state; how to beat the enemy and build an empire; how to lead wisely; and how to manoeuvre brilliantly.

Gems of Chinese Wisdom: Mastering the Art of Leadership
Translated by Leong Weng Kam
    Wise up with this delightful collection of tales and anecdotes on the wisdom of great men and women in Chinese history, including Confucius, Meng Changjun and Gou Jian.

Three Strategies of Huang Shi Gong: The Art of Government
Translated by Alan Chong
    Reputedly one of man's oldest monograph on military strategy, it unmasks the secrets behind brilliant military manoeuvres, clever deployment and control of subordinates, and effective government.

100 Strategies of War: Brilliant Tactics in Action
Translated by Yeo Ai Hoon
    The book captures the essence of extensive military knowledge and practice, and explores the use of psychology in warfare, the importance of building diplomatic relations with the enemy's neighbours, the use of espionage and reconnaissance, etc.

Asiapac Comic Series (by Tsai Chih Chung)

Art of War
Translated by Leong Weng Kam
   The Art of War provides a compact set of principles essential for victory in battles; applicable to military strategists, in business and human relationships.

Book of Zen
Translated by Koh Kok Kiang
   Zen makes the art of spontaneous living the prime concern of the human being. Tsai depicts Zen with unfettered versatility; his illustrations spans a period of more than 2,000 years.

Da Xue
Translated by Mary Ng En Tzu
   The second book in the Four Books of the Confucian Classics. It sets forth the higher principles of moral science and advocates that the cultivation of the person be the first thing attended to in the process of the pacification of kingdoms.

Fantasies of the Six Dynasties
Translated by Jenny Lim
   Tsai Chih Chung has creatively illustrated and annotated 19 bizarre tales of human encounters with supernatural beings which were compiled during the Six Dyansties (AD 220-589).

Lun Yu
Translated by Mary Ng En Tzu
   A collection of the discourses of Confucius, his disciples and others on various topics. Several bits of choice sayings have been illustrated for readers in this book.

New Account of World Tales
Translated by Alan Chong
   These 120 selected anecdotes tell the stories of emperors, princes, high officials, generals, courtiers, urbane monks and lettered gentry of a turbulent time. They afford a stark and amoral insight into human behaviour in its full spectrum of virtues and frailties and glimpses of brilliant Chinese witticisms, too.

Origins of Zen
Translated by Koh Kok Kiang
   Tsai in this book traces the origins and development of Zen in China with a light-hearted touch which is very much in keeping with the Zen spirit of absolute freedom and unbounded creativity.

Records of the Historian
Translated by Tang Nguok Kiong
   Adapted from Records of the Historian, one of the greatest historical work China has produced, Tsai has illustrated the life and characteristics of the Four Lords of the Warring Strates.

Roots of Wisdom
Translated by Koh Kok Kiang
   One of the gems of Chinese literature, whose advocacy of a steadfast nature and a life of simplicity, goodness, quiet joy and harmony with one's fellow beings and the world at large has great relevance in an age of rapid changes.

Sayings of Confucius
Translated by Goh Beng Choo
   This book features the life of Confucius, selected sayings from The Analects and some of his more prominent pupils. It captures the warm relationship between the sage and his disciples, and offers food for thought for the modern readers.

Sayings of Han Fei Zi
Translated by Alan Chong
   Tsai Chih Chung retold and interpreted the basic ideas of legalism, a classical political philosophy that advocates a draconian legal code, embodying a system of liberal reward and heavy penalty as the basis of government, in his unique style.

Sayings of Lao Zi
Translated by Koh Kok Kiang & Wong Lit Khiong
   The thoughts of Lao Zi, the founder of Taoism, are presented here in a light-hearted manner. It features the selected sayings from Dao De Jing.

Sayings of Lao Zi Book 2
Translated by Koh Kok Kiang

In the second book, Tsai Chih Chung has tackled some of the more abstruse passages from the Dao De Jing which he has not included in the first volume of Sayings of Lao Zi.

Sayings of Lie Zi
Translated by Koh Kok Kiang

A famous Taoist sage whose sayings deals with universal themes such as the joy of living, reconciliation with death, the limitations of human knowledge, the role of chance events.

Sayings of Mencius
Translated by Mary Ng En Tzu

This book contains stories about the life of Mencius and various excerpts from "Mencius", one of the Four Books of the Confucian Classics, which contains the philosophy of Mencius.

Sayings of Zhuang Zi
Translated by Goh Beng Choo

Zhuang Zi's non-conformist and often humorous views of life have been creatively illustrated and simply presented by Tsai Chih Chung in this book.

Sayings of Zhuang Zi Book 2
Translated by Koh Kok Kiang

Zhuang Zi's book is valued for both its philosophical insights and as a work of great literary merit. Tsai's second book on Zhuang Zi shows maturity in his unique style.

Strange Tales of Liaozhai
Translated by Tang Nguok Kiong

In this book, Tsai Chih Chung has creatively illustrated 12 stories from the Strange Tales of Liaozhai, an outstanding Chinese classic written by Pu Songling in the early Qing Dynasty.

Zhong Yong
Translated by Mary Ng En Tzu

Zhong Yong, written by Zi Si, the grandson of Confucius, gives voice to the heart of the discipline of Confucius. Tsai has presented it in a most readable manner for the modern readers to explore with great delight.

Hilarious Chinese Classics by Tsai Chih Chung

Journey to the West 1

These books offer more than the all-too-familiar escapades of Tan Sanzang and his animal disciples. Under the creative pen of Tsai Chih Chung, *Journey to the West* still stays its course but takes a new route. En route from ancient China to India to acquire Buddhist scriptures, the Monk and his disciples veer off course frequently to dart into modern times to have fleeting exchanges with characters ranging from Ronald Reagan to Bunny Girls of the Playboy Club.

Journey to the West 2

Romance of the Three Kingdoms

Set in the turbulent Three Kingdoms Period, *Romance of the Three Kingdoms* relates the clever political manoeuvres and brilliant battle strategies used by the ambitious rulers as they fought one another for supremacy.

In this comic version, Tsai Chih Chung has illustrated in an entertaining way the four best-known episodes in the novel. Don't be surprised to see a warrior waving an Iraqi flag, a satellite dish fixed on top of an ancient Chinese building, and court officials playing mahjong or eating beef noodles, a favourite Taiwanese snack.

Asiapac Comic Series : Contemporary Humour

Battle Domestica

A satire about married life typified by a middle-aged couple who derive sadistic pleasure from mutual verbal assault.

Known as *Double Big Guns* in Taiwan, its Chinese edition has sold more than 400,000 copies worldwide.

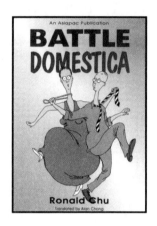

Sour Pack

There exist among us people who participate but are never committed; who are willing to give but attach more importance to what they get in return; who long for love but are terrified of being tied down.

Images of these people, their credo, and their lifestyles are reflected in the book. You may find in these cartoon characters familiar glimpses of yourself or those around you.

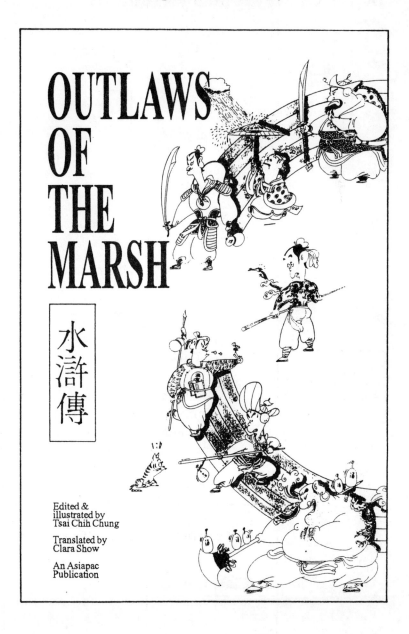

OUTLAWS OF THE MARSH

水滸傳

Edited &
illustrated by
Tsai Chih Chung

Translated by
Clara Show

An Asiapac
Publication

《亞太漫畫系列》

太監傳奇

編劇：王庸聲、池聲

漫畫：田恆玉

翻譯：楊愛文

亞太圖書有限公司出版